ALL ABOARD!

HIGH-SPEED TRAINS

by Nikki Bruno Clapper

Consulting Editor: Gail Saunders-Smith, PhD

Content Consultant: Martin Wachs, PhD
Professor Emeritus, Department of Urban Planning
University of California, Los Angeles

Pebble® Plus

raintree
a Capstone company — publishers for children

Raintree is an imprint of Capstone Global Library Limited, a company incorporated in England and Wales having its registered office at 7 Pilgrim Street, London EC4V 6LB – Registered company number: 6695582

www.raintree.co.uk
myorders@raintree.co.uk

Edited by Nikki Bruno Clapper and Linda Staniford
Designed by Juliette Peters
Picture research by Jo Miller
Production by Kathy McColley

ISBN 978 1 474 70183 9
19 18 17 16 15
10 9 8 7 6 5 4 3 2 1

British Library Cataloguing in Publication Data
A full catalogue record for this book is available from the British Library.

Acknowledgements
We would like to thank the following for permission to reproduce photographs:
Alamy: age fotostock, 5; Bernd Mellmann, 13, Peter Bowater, 9; Dreamstime: Iloveharbin, 15, Pedro Antonio Salaverria Calahorra, 7, Sébastien Bonaimé, 11; Newscom: EPA/Feng Iel, 1, EPA/Shen Yu, 21, Universal Images Group/JTB Photo, 19, ZUMA Press/Stefan Rousseau, 17; Shutterstock: hxdyl, 2-3, 22-23, Oleksiy Mark, cover (train), Petrovic Igor, cover (ticket), tovovan, train design element, (throughout)

Every effort has been made to contact copyright holders of material reproduced in this book. Any omissions will be rectified in subsequent printings if notice is given to the publisher.

All the internet addresses (URLs) given in this book were valid at the time of going to press. However, due to the dynamic nature of the internet, some addresses may have changed, or sites may have changed or ceased to exist since publication. While the author and publisher regret any inconvenience this may cause readers, no responsibility for any such changes can be accepted by either the author or the publisher.

Printed in China.

Contents

Whoosh!

The platform is full.

You hear a quiet *whoosh*.

A long white carriage appears.

The high-speed train is here!

High-speed trains whisk riders between large cities. They travel at 200 kilometres (125 miles) per hour or faster. All aboard!

Travel in comfort

High-speed trains are clean and comfortable. They have toilets and restaurant cars. Business travellers can plug in their computers.

Today there are high-speed
trains in Europe and Asia.
The United States and
Canada are planning to
have them too.

a high-speed train in France

11

It's electric

High-speed trains run
on electricity. Special tracks
help them move quickly.
Maglev trains use magnets
to float above the track.

Many people choose between high-speed trains and aeroplanes. These two vehicles compete to keep travel times and prices low.

Spotlight: Eurostar

The Eurostar travels from London to Paris in 2 hours and 20 minutes. It goes through a 50-kilometre (30-mile) tunnel under the English Channel.

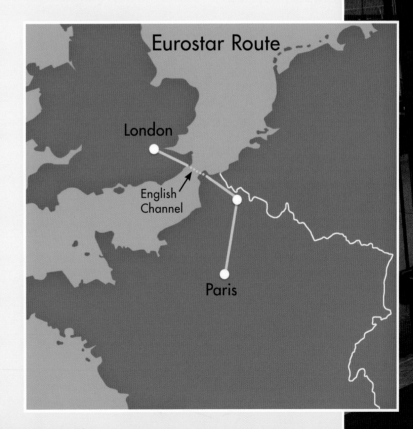

Eurostar Route

London

English Channel

Paris

Spotlight: bullet trains of Asia

Japan's high-speed trains are called bullet trains because they are so fast. E5 and E6 bullet trains can travel at 322 kilometres (200 miles) per hour.

The world's fastest train is the maglev in Shanghai, China. It can rush along at 431 kilometres (268 miles) per hour.

GLOSSARY

carriage one of the wheeled vehicles that are put together to form a train

compete try hard to outdo others

electricity natural force that can be used to make light and heat or to make machines work

high-speed train train that travels at a speed of 125 miles (200 kilometres) per hour or faster

maglev train train that uses magnets to glide above the track

magnet material or object that creates an area of electrical currents that affects other objects

platform raised, flat surface; people stand on platforms to wait for trains

track rail or set of rails for vehicles such as trains and trolleys to run on

whisk move or carry quickly

vehicle something that carries people or goods from one place to another

FIND OUT MORE

Books

Bullet Trains (Fast!), Ian Graham (QED, 2010)

Bullet Trains (Now That's Fast), Kate Riggs (Franklin Watts, 2011)

Websites

Find out lots of facts about trains:

http://primaryfacts.com/4645/train-facts-for-kids

Learn more about all kinds of trains:

http://easyscienceforkids.com/all-about-trains

INDEX